CARB CYCLING FOR WOMEN OVER 50

Easy Guide for Weight Loss & Optimal Health With
Easy-to-Follow Steps for High Carb & Low Card Days,
Delicious Recipes to Boost Metabolism & Stay
Energized.

Vince Cruise Sant

"Discover vibrant health and renewed vitality with 'Carb Cycling for Women Over 40.' We dig into the transforming realm of carb cycling in this inspiring book, designed exclusively for women on the path to greater health. Discover how to use carbs intelligently, accept flexibility, and create a thoughtful approach to fueling your body and spirit".

ABOUT THE AUTHOR

Introducing Vince Cruise Sant, a seasoned nutritionist with over a decade of dedicated experience in transforming lives through the power of balanced nutrition. With an extensive background in the field, Vince has emerged as a respected figure, dedicated to guiding individuals toward achieving their health and wellness aspirations.

With a wealth of practical knowledge and a deep understanding of nutrition and metabolism, Vince's expertise extends beyond theory. Having positively impacted the lives of more than 300 individuals, he stands as a testament to the tangible results his guidance brings.

Vince's approach transcends the conventional, recognizing the individuality of each person's journey toward well-being. His methodology seamlessly blends scientific insights with real-world application, ensuring that his advice is not only attainable but also sustainable.

Recognized as a trusted advisor and advocate for balanced nutrition, Vince Cruise Sant's commitment to empowering individuals is unwavering. His reputation as a compassionate and knowledgeable guide underscores his dedication to helping others unlock their full potential.

Whether you're a newcomer to the path of wellness or seeking to refine your existing practices, Vince's expertise will inspire and educate. Prepare to embark on a transformative journey led by a visionary who firmly believes that vibrant health is an achievable reality. With Vince's guidance, your pursuit of lasting well-being is poised for exceptional success.

TABLE OF CONTENTS

INTRODUCTION

Welcome to a journey of health, energy, and strength that will change your life. As women, we go through a lot of changes in our lives, and when we reach our 40s and beyond, our bodies start a new chapter of change. This is a time when we gain knowledge, experience, and a deep understanding of who we are, but our bodies may also seem to have a mind of their own.

If you're reading this, you've already started looking for overall well-being and have come to a very important crossroads. Here, you'll find a way to lose weight that isn't just another diet. Instead, it's a way that fits the unique needs of women over 40. This method, my dear readers, is called sugar cycling. It is a powerful way to eat that works with the rhythm of your body, giving you more energy and helping you reach your health and fitness goals.

You might ask, "Why carb cycling? Because as women over 40, we're not just looking for surface changes. We want to be healthy in our bodies, minds, and emotions for the long term. Hormones make our bodies move like a symphony, and sugar cycling is like the director, making sure everything is in balance and giving us amazing results.

In the pages that follow, we'll talk more about the science behind carb cycling and how it works perfectly with a woman's body. We'll bust some myths, talk about the problems, and, most importantly, enjoy the wins that are still to come. This isn't about a quick fix or a change that happens quickly. It's about accepting a way of life that hugs you back.

Get ready to learn, change, and grow as we go through the process of tailoring your food intake to your goals and hormone rhythm. We'll talk about how to make meals that give you energy, how to deal with plateaus, and how to make carb cycling a natural part of your daily life.

But this isn't a trip for one person. These pages are full of advice from women just like you—women who have had the same fears, hopes, and questions. Their stories, thoughts, and successes will give you hope and let you know that you're not the only one who wants to be healthy in every way.

So, whether you're an exercise fan who wants to change up your routine, a busy worker who wants to keep your energy up, or a woman who wants to be her best self, carb cycling has a way for you. Let's start this journey of change together, one turn at a time. Welcome to "Carb

Cycling for Women Over 40," a guide to glowing health and a celebration of your amazing journey.

CHAPTER ONE

FUNDAMENTALS OF CARB CYCLING

What is Carb Cycling?

Carb cycling is a way to plan your diet in which you eat different amounts of carbs on different days or at different times of the week. It's not a one-size-fits-all idea. Instead, it's a fluid and personalized approach that can be changed to fit each person's goals, habits, and bodily reactions.

At its core, carb cycling is based on the idea that carbs are important for feeding our bodies and helping them do different things. But our bodies' needs for carbs can change depending on things like how active we are, our digestion, changes in hormones, and our exercise goals. Carb cycling takes advantage of this variation to improve energy levels, speed up fat loss, and boost muscle growth while reducing the negative effects of a high-carb or low-carb diet that doesn't change.

"High carb" days are days when you eat more carbs than usual; "moderate carb" days are days when you eat more carbs than usual; and "low carb" days are days when you eat less carbs than usual. Each person can change how and when these days happen based on their own interests and goals.

How the Carb Cycling Process Works:

1. Days with a lot of carbs: On days when you want to eat more carbs, you do so on purpose. This gives your body enough energy for hard workouts, refills glycogen stores (the form of carbs stored in muscles), and helps your metabolism work as a whole.

2. Low Carb Days: On low carb days, you limit the amount of carbs you eat. This makes your body more likely to use fat for energy, which helps you lose weight. Also, eating fewer carbs can help keep insulin levels in check, which may improve insulin sensitivity.

3. Days with moderate carbs: These days are a good mix of high-carb and low-carb days. They can give you steady energy for light tasks and workouts while also helping your body burn fat.

Specifically for women over 40:

What makes carb cycling different is that it can be changed to fit the needs of women over 40. As hormones change during this time of life, the body's energy and makeup can also change. Carb cycling can be changed to deal with these changes by adjusting the carbohydrate diet to match changes in hormones. This makes it easier to control weight, mood, and energy levels.

How Carb Cycling Works

Carb cycling is based on the idea that you should plan how many carbs you eat to give you the most energy, help you reach your fitness goals, and speed up your fat burning. By switching between eating a lot of carbs, a little carbs, and a reasonable amount of carbs, you can build a healthy rhythm that fits the needs of your body on different days.

1. Days with a lot of carbs:

On "high carb" days, you do it on purpose to eat more carbohydrates. This large amount of carbs serves a few purposes:

How to Fuel Workouts: Carbohydrates are the main source of energy for your body, especially when you're working out hard. On days when you eat a lot of carbs, your muscles will have enough energy to get through tough workouts.

Helping your muscles grow: Carbohydrates help save protein, which means they stop muscle tissue from being broken down to make energy. This is especially important if you want to gain and keep lean muscle mass.

Increasing your metabolism: A brief rise in carbohydrate intake can help the thyroid make more hormones and keep the metabolism from slowing down, which could happen if you cut calories for a long time.

2. Low-Carb Days: On low-carb days, you eat fewer carbs, which makes your body use more of its fat stores for energy. This helps you lose fat and has other benefits:

Adaptation to Fat: When you eat fewer carbs, your body uses the fat it has stored for energy. Over time, this can make it easier for your body to use fat as fuel, which can help you lose weight.

Controlling Insulin: Getting less carbs helps keep blood sugar levels steady and can make insulin work better. This is especially helpful for people who have trouble with insulin or are trying to lose weight.

Controlling your appetite: Protein- and fat-rich meals on low-carb days tend to fill you up more, which helps you control your hunger and eat less overall.

3. Days with some carbs:

Moderate-carb days are a happy medium between high-carb days and days with few carbs. They give you a steady supply of carbs that you can use to:

Help moderate activities: On days when you don't work out hard, a modest amount of carbs gives you steady energy for daily tasks and light exercise.

Hormone Balance: For women, days with a reasonable amount of carbs can help control hormones like cortisol and thyroid hormones, which helps keep hormones in balance generally.

Changing the way women over 40 ride carb bikes

Hormonal changes can change a woman's metabolism, mood, and energy level after she turns 40. Carb cycling can be changed to deal with the following:

Things to think about during menopause: Changing the amount of carbs you eat based on your period or stage of menopause can help you deal with symptoms like hot flashes, mood swings, and weight changes.

Managing your metabolism: Carb cycling can help keep your metabolism from slowing down as you get older, which is good for your health.

Optimizing energy use: By adjusting the amount of carbs you eat, you can make sure you have enough energy throughout the day and avoid feeling tired or slow.

Types of Carb Cycling Approaches

1. High/Low Carb Days:

One of the most common ways to carb cycle is to switch between days with a lot of carbs and days with fewer carbs. This method works best for people who want to find a balance between hard workouts and helping them lose fat. Let's look more closely at how the high carb/low carb days method works:

Days with a lot of carbs:

On days when you want to eat more carbs, you do so on purpose. These days are planned to go with the days when you work out the hardest or are the busiest.

1. Keeping up with workouts: For high-intensity tasks, the body gets most of its energy from carbohydrates. By eating more carbs on these days, you make sure your muscles have enough energy, which makes your workouts more effective and last longer.

2. Muscle Growth: Days with a lot of carbs help muscles heal and grow. By eating more carbs, you maintain your hard-earned muscle bulk and keep protein from being used for energy.

3. Boost your metabolism: Some hormones, like thyroid hormones and leptin, that help regulate the metabolism and control hunger can rise when you eat more carbs for a short time.

Carb-free days:

On low-carb days, you eat a lot less carbs than usual. Most of the time, these days are followed by rest days or days with less intense workouts.

1. How fat is used: Your body gets more energy from stored fat when you eat fewer carbs. This helps you lose fat and makes your metabolism better at burning fat.

2. Managing insulin: If you eat fewer carbs, you can keep insulin levels in check. This can make insulin work better and help control blood sugar better, which is important for managing weight and staying healthy overall.

3. Controlling your appetite: On low-carb days, foods with a lot of protein and a modest amount of fat can help you control your hunger and stop you from eating too much, which makes it easier to stay in a calorie deficit.

Customizing Low-Carb and High-Carb Days for Women Over 40:

Changes in hormones can have a big effect on how your body reacts to carbs if you are a woman over 40. Think about these changes:

1. Balance of hormones: Make days when you eat a lot of carbs fit in with your period or menopause. Change the amount of carbs you eat to help control biological changes and the symptoms that come with them.

2. Energy and mood: Plan your high-carb days so that you have steady energy and a good mood, especially when your hormones are changing and you might feel tired or have mood changes.

3. Support for your metabolism: Days with a lot of carbs can stop your metabolism from slowing down as you get older by quickly speeding it up. This helps you maintain a better metabolism.

2. Weekly Carb Rotation:

In the carb cycle plan, the weekly carb exchange is another way that works well. The high-carb days/low-carb days method rotates between two different days. The weekly carb rotation method, on the other hand, includes going through different amounts of carbohydrates over the course of several days in a week. This change can be especially helpful for people who like to eat at a slower pace for longer periods of time.

The cycle of the week

With the weekly carb exchange method, you set up a cycle that lasts for a week. This cycle usually has three different days with different amounts of carbs:

1. Days with a lot of carbs: On "high carb" days, you eat more carbs than you do on other days. On these days, you probably do your hardest workouts or do other things that are hard on your body.

2. Moderate Carb Days: On moderate carb days, you eat a medium amount of carbs. These days are good for working out regularly and being busy.

3. Days with few carbs: On low-carb days, you eat fewer carbs than usual. These days might fall on days when people rest or do less strenuous physical tasks.

Benefits of switching up your carbs every week:

1. When to eat food: With the weekly carb cycle method, you can time your higher carbohydrate intake to coincide with your workouts, giving your body the fuel, it needs to perform well.

2. Metabolic Flexibility: Cycling through different amounts of carbohydrate helps your body get better at using different energy sources, like carbs and fats, in different ways.

3. Sustainability: Some people may be able to stick with the plan better if they eat a range of carbs. It gives you freedom and doesn't require you to keep track of high- and low-carb days every day.

Changing the rotation of carbs for women over 40:

1. Things to think about with hormones: As a woman over 40, you might want to change the time of your high-carb days to match the changes in your hormones. This can help you feel better and have more energy during different parts of your period or menopause.

2. Your body's metabolism and age: The weekly sugar exchange method can help fight the effects of aging on the metabolism by making the metabolism more flexible and stopping it from adapting to a single eating pattern.

3. Long-Term Wellness: Use this method to set up a healthy eating routine that will last and support your general health and fitness goals, taking into account the special needs and challenges that women over 40 experiences.

3. Daily Calorie and Carb Variance:

The technique of changing the number of calories and carbs you eat every day is a fluid and changing part of the carb cycling plan. With this method, you change how many calories and carbs you eat each day based on how active you are and what you want to accomplish that day. It can be changed in more ways and responds better to your body's changing needs

Personalized adjustments every day:

In this method, you change the number of calories you eat and the amount of carbs you eat every day based on the following factors:

1. The level of activity: When you're busier, like when you're working out, you need more carbs to keep you going and help you heal.

2. Days of rest or light activity: On days when you don't do as much, you cut back on carbs to match the smaller amount of energy you use.

Difference in Calories and Carbs:

1. Days with a lot of calories and carbs: You eat more calories and carbs on days when you work out hard or do other physically demanding things. This helps with energy, efficiency, and healing.

2. Days with a Medium Amount of Calories and Carbs: You eat a modest amount of calories and carbs on days when you don't do much. This gives you enough energy without giving you too much.

3. Days with Few Calories and Carbs: On days when you rest or don't do much physical exercise, you eat fewer calories and carbs. This keeps people from eating too many calories while still giving them the nutrients they need.

Benefits of a daily variation in calories and carbs:

1. Accuracy: This method lets you make changes in real time based on what your body needs, making sure you get the right amount of energy and carbs every day.

2. Energy Balance: When you match the number of calories you eat with the number of calories you burn, you maintain a better energy balance, which is important for weight control and general health.

3. Flexible Lifestyle: The daily variety method can work with different plans and activities, so it's good for people who have busy, unpredictable lives.

Changing the daily number of calories and carbs for women over 40:

1. Things to think about with hormones and menopause: Women over 40 should think about how hormone changes affect them and change how much carbohydrate they eat to keep hormones in balance and relieve symptoms.

2. Energy Optimization: Changing the amount of carbs you eat based on how much energy you need and how your hormones change can boost your energy and general health.

3. Health in the long run: The daily variation method can help you develop a healthy eating plan that fits your changing needs as you get older. This is good for your health and happiness in the long run.

CHAPTER TWO

TAILORING CARB CYCLING TO WOMEN OVER 40

Hormonal Changes and Metabolism After 40

When women reach their 40s and beyond, they go through a big change in their hormones, which is mostly caused by perimenopause and menopause. These changes can have a big effect on the body's energy, shape, and general health. Understanding these changes is important if you want to use nutrition tactics, like sugar cycling, to help women's health at this time in their lives.

Perimenopause and menopause are changes in hormones:

1. The drop in estrogen: One of the most noticeable changes is that the body makes less estrogen. Estrogen is a hormone that affects a woman's ability to have children. It also affects the body's metabolism, bone health, and mood.

2. Changes in progesterone: Progesterone levels may also go down, which can change the menstrual cycle and cause signs like unpredictable periods, mood swings, and changes in how you sleep.

3. How it affects your metabolism: Estrogen helps control the rate of metabolism and the way fat is distributed in the body. Its loss can cause changes in how the body stores and uses energy, which could cause weight gain, especially around the stomach.

Changes in the body's chemistry after 40

1. A slower metabolism: As you get older, your metabolism slows down on its own because of things like muscle loss (sarcopenia) and changes in hormones. This can cause a slow drop in the amount of energy you use every day.

2. Muscle Mass: As people get older, they tend to lose muscle mass, which can change their basal metabolic rate (BMR). When you have less muscle, your basal metabolic rate (BMR) goes down, which means you burn fewer calories when you're not doing anything.

3. Sensitivity to insulin: Insulin sensitivity may go down, which makes it harder for the body to use glucose (sugar) as a source of energy. This can make you gain weight and make you more likely to develop insulin resistance or type 2 diabetes.

4. The redistribution of fat: Hormonal changes can cause a change in where fat is stored, with more fat being stored around the belly. This abdominal fat makes you more likely to develop metabolic diseases.

In terms of carb cycling and nutrition, this means:

Understanding these hormonal and metabolic changes is important for women over 40 who want to use diet plans like carb cycling.

1. Making changes: Know that changes in your hormones can change how your body reacts to food. Adjust your diet to keep your hormones in balance and prevent weight gain.

2. Nutrient Density: Focus on foods that are high in nutrients to help your bones stay healthy (calcium and vitamin D), keep your muscles in good shape (protein), and make hormones (healthy fats).

3. Balanced Approach: Eat the right amount of carbs, proteins, and fats to keep your energy up and your muscles strong.

4. Hydration: Changes in hormones can affect how much water a person needs. Staying well hydrated is good for your metabolism and general health.

5. Lifestyle factors: Make sleep, managing stress, and frequent physical exercise a priority to help your metabolism and hormone balance.

Customizing Carb Intake for Hormonal Balance

As a woman over 40, you have a thorough awareness of your body's subtleties. Using this information to tailor your carbohydrate consumption may have a significant influence on your hormonal balance, energy levels, and general well-being. Here's how you can customize your carb consumption to promote hormonal balance:

Considerations for the Menstrual Cycle:

Understanding the stages of your cycle will help you enhance your carb cycling diet if you still have menstrual cycles.

1. Follicular Period: Estrogen levels rise throughout the first half of your cycle (days 1–14). This is an excellent time to include more complex carbohydrates since they may aid in serotonin synthesis, therefore improving mood and energy.

Luteal Period: Progesterone levels increase in the second part of your cycle (days 15–28). This may improve insulin sensitivity, allowing your body to use carbs more efficiently. Maintain a balanced carbohydrate intake and control cravings.

2. Menopausal Concerns: Adapting your food consumption to handle hormonal shifts becomes even more important for women moving into or through menopause.

Sensitivity to Insulin: Focus on controlling insulin sensitivity when estrogen levels fall. To avoid blood sugar spikes, prioritize complex carbs and fiber-rich diets.

Bone Wellness: A sufficient carbohydrate intake promotes calcium absorption and bone health. Consider including nutrient-dense whole grains and veggies.

Energy and Mood: Balanced carbohydrate consumption promotes serotonin synthesis, which may improve mood and energy while combating mood swings and weariness.

3. Individual Difference: Every woman's body reacts differently to hormonal fluctuations. Pay attention to your body's indications and modify your carbohydrate intake as needed.

Amounts of Energy: Keep track of how varied carbohydrate amounts affect your energy levels throughout the day. Adjust as required to maintain consistent energy levels.

Desires: Carb cycling may aid with desire management. Adjust carbohydrate consumption on particular days to avoid overindulgence.

Digestive Health: For gut health, focus on high-fiber carbs. Adequate fiber consumption promotes hormone metabolism and helps alleviate the symptoms of hormonal swings.

4. Consulting Experts: Consult a healthcare physician or trained dietician if you have particular health issues or are using drugs. They may provide specific advice to ensure that your carb cycling diet is in line with your health objectives.

Addressing Menopausal Challenges with Carb Cycling

Menopause is a normal stage in a woman's life that marks the end of her reproductive years and is generally accompanied by a slew of hormonal and physiological changes. These modifications may have an effect on your metabolism, energy levels, and general well-being. Carb cycling is an effective way to manage menopausal issues and boost your health during this transitional period.

1. Hormonal Changes:

Estrogen Reduction: As estrogen levels fall, you may experience hot flashes, mood fluctuations, and weight gain. Modifying carbohydrate consumption may assist in attenuating these effects.

Sensitivity to Insulin: Insulin sensitivity may be affected by hormonal changes. Adjust carbohydrate consumption to maintain steady blood sugar levels and avoid energy dumps.

2. Weight Control:

Metabolism: During menopause, the metabolism slows down. Carb cycling may aid in weight loss by optimizing energy intake on active days and encouraging fat utilization on low-carb days.

Fat in the Abdomen: Increased fat buildup around the abdomen may be caused by hormonal changes. Carb cycling, particularly on low-carb days, may target visceral fat and aid in weight loss.

3. Energy and Mood:

Serotonin Production: A balanced carbohydrate intake promotes serotonin production, which regulates mood and aids in the treatment of mood swings, anxiety, and irritability that are prevalent during menopause.

Sustained Energy: Adjusting carbohydrate intake depending on activity level and hormonal variations delivers sustained energy throughout the day, alleviating weariness.

4. Bone Health:

Nutrient-Dense Carbohydrates: Include nutrient-dense carbohydrate foods that are high in vitamins and minerals that promote bone health, which is especially essential during menopause.

5. Hot Flashes and Sleep Disruptions:

Blood Sugar Control: Blood sugar spikes and decreases may cause hot flashes and disrupt sleep. You might possibly lessen these symptoms by reducing your carbohydrate consumption.

6. Seek the advice of a healthcare professional:

If you're experiencing particular menopausal symptoms, talk to your doctor or a certified nutritionist. They can assist you in customizing your carb cycling strategy to meet your specific demands and health objectives.

7. Mindful Self-Care:

Aside from carb cycling, emphasize self-care strategies like stress management, frequent physical exercise, and enough sleep. These variables are critical in dealing with menopausal symptoms.

8. Monitoring and Adjustment:

Keep a notebook to keep track of how various carb cycling methods affect your symptoms, energy levels, and general well-being. Use this data to make educated changes to your strategy.

CHAPTER THREE

CREATING A CARB CYCLING PLAN

Setting Clear Goals

When developing a carb cycling strategy, it is critical to have clear and well-defined targets. Every part of your plan will be guided by your objectives, from selecting the best carb cycling technique to establishing the allocation of high, moderate, and low carb days. Setting specific targets may assist you in developing an effective and customized carb cycling plan.

1. Clarity of Goal:

Setting objectives helps you understand what you want to accomplish with carb cycling. Having a specific objective offers direction and purpose, whether it's weight reduction, muscle building, increased energy, or better hormonal balance.

2. Customizing Your Approach:

Different techniques are required for different purposes. For example, if fat reduction is your main aim, your carb cycling strategy may include extra low-carb days to boost fat use. If you want to grow muscle, you should concentrate on high-carb days to fuel your tough exercises.

3. Developing a Roadmap:

Goals serve as a road map for structuring your carb cycling approach in the short and long run. Knowing where you're going helps you establish goals and monitor your progress.

4. Intensity Determination:

The severity of your carb cycling strategy is determined by your objectives. More aggressive objectives may call for more frequent low-carb days, while less aggressive goals may call for a more balanced mix of high, moderate, and low-carb days.

5. Measurement and Evaluation:

Clear objectives provide demonstrable results. You may monitor your success by evaluating changes in weight, body composition, energy levels, and other pertinent indicators, depending on your objectives.

6. Motivation and Concentration:

Goals keep you engaged and motivated. Having a goal to strive towards improves consistency and commitment to your carb cycling approach.

7. Expectations that are realistic:

Setting specific objectives allows you to set reasonable expectations. Understanding what is feasible within a given period reduces frustration and supports a long-term perspective.

8. Adapting as Necessary:

As you develop, you may discover that your objectives change. Having specific goals helps you modify your carb cycling strategy to meet your shifting goals.

9. Psychological Advantages:

Reaching your objectives gives you a feeling of achievement and enhances your confidence. These psychological advantages may improve your general well-being.

10. Personalization:

Goals personalize your carb cycling strategy. Instead of taking a cookie-cutter approach, you're customizing your strategy to your own goals and tastes.

11. Long-Term Goals:

Clear objectives go beyond your current strategy. They assist you in seeing the larger picture of your health and fitness journey, helping you even after you've achieved your first goals.

Determining Daily Caloric Needs

Understanding your daily calorie requirements is a critical step in developing an efficient carb cycling diet. The quantity of calories you eat is critical to meeting your health and fitness objectives.

1. Creating a Baseline:

Identifying your daily calorie requirements offers a foundation for your carb cycling strategy. It teaches you how much energy your body needs to maintain its present weight and function.

2. Setting Objectives:

The quantity of calories you need will be influenced by your objectives, whether they be weight reduction, muscle growth, or maintenance. Weight reduction requires a calorie deficit, but muscle building requires a caloric excess.

3. Caloric Control:

Carb cycling entails varying carbohydrate consumption on various days. Knowing your daily caloric demands helps you alter carb consumption while remaining within your total energy requirements.

4. Individualization:

Variable carb cycling strategies (high/low days, weekly rotation, daily variation) have varying effects on calorie intake. Knowing your calorie requirements allows you to choose a strategy that fits your objectives and tastes.

5. Providing Adequate Nutrition:

Caloric requirements affect not just weight but also food intake. You guarantee that you acquire enough necessary nutrients for good health by satisfying your calorie demands.

6. Preventing Excessive Restrictions:

Knowing your daily calorie demands helps you avoid unnecessarily restricted diets, which may be harmful in the long term. It is critical to strike the proper balance between energy intake and expenditure.

7. Reducing Excessive Consumption:

On high-carb days, it's critical to limit calorie intake to prevent stifling growth. Knowing your caloric requirements allows you to manage your carbohydrate consumption without exceeding your energy requirements.

8. Progress Monitoring:

Tracking your calorie intake in relation to your requirements helps you measure your progress. If you aren't getting the results you want, you may change your strategy depending on your calorie consumption.

9. Long-Term Approach:

Creating a carb cycling regimen that corresponds to your calorie requirements encourages sustainability. A strategy that suits your energy needs is more likely to be pleasant and simple to follow.

10. Evolution Over Time:

Your calorie requirements may alter as your objectives or exercise levels change. Being aware of this dynamic nature allows you to modify your carb cycling strategy as required.

11. Professional Advice:

A trained dietitian or nutritionist may help you determine your calorie requirements more accurately. They may take into account a variety of characteristics to deliver customized suggestions.

Structuring High, Low, and Moderate Carb Days

A well-designed carb cycling regimen incorporates high, low, and moderate carb days. This smart carbohydrate intake arrangement serves as the basis for accomplishing your health and fitness objectives

1. Taking Advantage of Energy Demands:

- **High Carbohydrate Days:** Align your high-carb days with your most strenuous exercises or physically active days. Increased carbohydrate consumption provides the energy required for performance and recuperation.

- **Moderate Carbohydrate Days:** These days are ideal for moderate activity and frequent exercise. They provide a healthy quantity of carbs to keep energy levels up.

- **Low Carbohydrate Days:** Low-carb days should be reserved for rest days or days with little physical activity. Your body now depends more on stored fat for energy, encouraging fat utilization.

2. Hormonal Harmony:

- **Pre-menopausal Women's Cycle Phases:** If you're still menstruating, organize your carb cycling around the stages of your menstrual cycle.

Low-carb days during the luteal phase may help control cravings and energy swings, while high-carb days during the follicular phase boost energy demands.

Menopausal Women's Hormonal Changes: To handle the hormonal fluctuations associated with menopause, tailor your high-carb days. Increase your carbohydrate consumption intelligently to improve your mood and energy during hormonal swings.

3. Fitness Objectives:

- **Loss of Fat:** Consider having more low-carb days to promote fat reduction. These days, fat consumption is encouraged and might result in a calorie deficit, which aids in weight reduction.

- **Muscle Growth:** Prioritize high-carb days around strength training sessions for muscle building. Carbohydrates provide energy throughout exercises and aid in muscle rehabilitation and development.

4. Progress and Adaptation:

- **Adaptation Variation:** Different carb days keep your body from adopting a particular pattern, which may stymie growth. It keeps your metabolism running smoothly.

- **Monitoring Progress:** Structured carb days enable you to see how your body reacts over time. Adjust your strategy depending on your progress, energy levels, and other indicators.

5. Long-Term Approach:

- **Balanced Nutrition:** Planning carb days ensures that your total diet is balanced and that you are getting the nutrients you need for health and well-being.

- **Avoiding Excessiveness:** By alternating carb days, you avoid excessive limitations that may result in binge eating or metabolic slowdown.

6. Individualization:

- **Perfect for Your Lifestyle:** Plan your carb days around your schedule and lifestyle. For example, high-carb days on busy exercise days and low-carb days on rest days

- **Listening to Your Body:** Notice how your body reacts to various carb days. Change the framework according to how you feel and perform.

7. Professional Counseling:

- **Seek Professional Advice:** If you're unclear about how to organize your carb days, consult with a licensed dietitian or nutritionist. They may provide tailored suggestions depending on your objectives and requirements.

Selecting the Right Carbohydrate Sources

Choosing the correct carbohydrate sources is critical to developing an effective and balanced carbohydrate cycling strategy. The type of carbs you consume has a significant impact on your energy levels, general nutrition, and how effectively your body reacts to carb cycling.

1. Nutrient Density:

- **Whole Grains:** Whole grains such as quinoa, brown rice, oats, and whole wheat bread are ideal. These are high in fiber, vitamins, and minerals, all of which benefit general health and digestion.
- **Legumes:** Include a variety of colorful veggies in your diet to acquire complex carbohydrates, vitamins, minerals, and antioxidants. They're rich in fiber and low in calories.

- **Fruits:** Fruits include natural carbohydrates, vitamins, and antioxidants. Combine them with protein and healthy fats for long-lasting energy.

2. Consistent Energy:

- **Complex Carbohydrates:** Concentrate on complex carbs that give long-lasting energy. Whole grains, legumes, and starchy vegetables are examples.
- **Fiber Composition:** Carbohydrates high in fiber, such as beans, lentils, and fibrous vegetables, release energy slowly, minimizing energy dips.

3. Blood Sugar Control:

- **GI (Glycemic Index):** To avoid blood sugar spikes and crashes, choose foods with a low to moderate glycemic index.
- **Carbohydrate Pairings:** To delay digestion and regulate blood sugar levels, combine carbs with protein, healthy fats, and fiber.

4. Nutritional Timing:

- **Before Workout:** To offer immediate energy before intensive exercises, use readily digestible carbohydrates like fruits or a modest quantity of complex carbs.

- **Post-Workout:** Choose fast-digesting carbohydrates and protein after workouts to restore glycogen reserves and boost muscle repair.

5. Hormonal Harmony:

- **Folate-Rich Carbohydrates:** Include folate-rich carbohydrates such as lentils, beans, and leafy greens throughout the luteal phase (for premenopausal women) to promote mood and hormonal balance.

- **B Vitamins:** Choose B vitamin-rich carbohydrates, such as whole grains and legumes, to help with energy metabolism and hormone balance.

6. Portion Management:

Caloric Consumption: Pay attention to portion sizes, particularly on days when you're eating a lot of carbs. Excess carbohydrate intake, even from high-quality sources, might stymie growth.

Well-Rounded Meals: Combine carbohydrates with proteins and healthy fats to make balanced meals that keep you full and avoid overeating.

7. Digestive Health:

Fiber Consumption: Fiber from carbohydrate sources is important for digestion, intestinal health, and hormone metabolism.

Hydration: Because fiber-rich carbohydrates absorb water, remain hydrated to avoid intestinal discomfort.

8. Customization:

Food Sensitivities: When choosing carbohydrate sources, keep any food sensitivities or allergies in mind.

Preferred Carbohydrate Sources: Select carbohydrate sources that you love. Variety ensures that you get a wide spectrum of nutrients.

9. Professional Counseling:

Seek the advice of a dietitian: Consult a certified nutritionist if you're unclear about which carbohydrate sources to include. They can assist you in tailoring your options to your individual objectives and requirements.

Incorporating Fiber and Micronutrients

Including fiber and micronutrients in your carb cycling strategy is a proactive way to improve your health, energy, and general well-being. These components are essential for digestion, hormone balance, and the proper functioning of your body.

1. Digestive Health:

- **Fiber-Rich Carbohydrates:** Fiber intake is increased by including whole grains, legumes, vegetables, and fruits in your diet. Fiber aids digestion, avoids constipation, and promotes gut health.

- **Regular Elimination:** Adequate fiber consumption promotes regular bowel movements, which reduce pain and promote overall well-being.

2. Satiety and Weight Control:

- **Complete and satisfying:** Carbohydrates high in fiber create a sensation of fullness and pleasure, lowering the probability of overeating and assisting with weight control.

- **Caloric Density:** Fiber-rich foods are frequently lower in calorie density, enabling you to eat larger quantities without overindulging.

3. Blood Sugar Control:

- **Consistent Energy:** Fiber slows carbohydrate digestion and absorption, resulting in a steady release of glucose into the circulation and stable energy levels.
- **Blood Sugar Spikes Reduced:** High-fiber diets may help minimize blood sugar spikes and crashes, resulting in improved energy management.

4. Micronutrient Supplementation:

- **Vitamins and Minerals:** Fruits, vegetables, and whole grains are high in vitamins and minerals that help with immune function, energy metabolism, and general health.
- **Antioxidants:** Micronutrients like vitamins C and E, as well as minerals like selenium and zinc, operate as antioxidants, shielding cells from oxidative stress damage.

5. Hormonal Harmony:

- **Magnesium and Vitamin B6:** Whole grains and leafy greens include vitamins that help manage mood and hormonal balance.

- **Folate:** Folate from sources such as legumes and greens is essential for DNA synthesis and cell repair, and it is also important for hormonal and general health.

6. Long-Term Health:

- **Bone Wellness:** Many fiber-rich carbohydrate sources include calcium and magnesium, which promote bone health and lower the risk of osteoporosis.
- **Cardiovascular Health:** Fiber consumption has been linked to lower cholesterol levels and a lower risk of heart disease.

7. Color and Variety:

- **Foods with Color:** A diverse selection of colored fruits and vegetables provides a variety of micronutrients and antioxidants.
- **Diverse Sources:** Include a variety of whole grains, legumes, veggies, and fruits to acquire a full range of nutrients.

8. Hydration:

- **Water Absorption:** Fiber absorbs water and helps to keep you hydrated. Drink plenty of water, particularly on high-fiber days.

9. Professional Counseling:

- **Seek the advice of a dietitian:** A licensed dietitian can provide specific advice if you're unclear about how to add fiber and micronutrients to your carb cycling regimen.

CHAPTER FOUR

WORKOUT NUTRITION AND CARB CYCLING

Pre-Workout Nutrition Strategies

1. Snack with Carbohydrates and Protein:

30–60 minutes before your exercise, eat a balanced snack that contains both carbs and protein. This combination delivers long-lasting energy and aids in muscle regeneration and recovery. Try a tiny apple with a spoonful of nut butter or a whole-grain rice cake with a piece of turkey, for example.

2. Low-glycemic carbohydrates with good fats:

Choose low-glycemic-index carbs with healthy fats. This combination helps to balance blood sugar levels and delivers long-lasting energy. Have a handful of mixed nuts with a modest dish of berries, for example.

3. Greek Yogurt Parfait

Enjoy a Greek yogurt parfait topped with mixed berries and granola. Greek yogurt is high in protein, while berries are high in vitamins, antioxidants, and carbs for energy. Choose granola that contains nutritious grains and has little added sugar.

4. Nut Butter Oatmeal:

A bowl of oats topped with nut butter and cinnamon is a delicious alternative. Oats give complex carbohydrates for energy, and nut butter adds healthy fats and protein to help you get through your exercise.

5. Electrolyte Hydration:

Keep hydrated before your exercise. If you're going to be active for an extended period of time, consider drinking a sports drink containing electrolytes. Electrolytes aid in fluid balance and avoid dehydration, which improves performance.

Post-Workout Nutrition Strategies

1. Protein-Packed Smoothie:

Make a protein-rich smoothie using protein powder, a banana, almond milk, and a handful of spinach. This combination contains amino acids that are necessary for muscle healing as well as carbs that replenish glycogen storage.

2. Quinoa Salad with Lean Protein:

A quinoa salad with lean protein sources like grilled chicken or tofu, as well as a range of bright veggies, is a great way to start the day. Quinoa has complex carbohydrates and protein, while veggies include vitamins and minerals that aid in recovery and general health.

3. Whole-Grain Wrap:

Make a whole grain wrap with lean protein (tuna, chicken, or beans), veggies, and a sprinkle of olive oil or hummus. The combination of protein and complex carbohydrates aids in muscle regeneration and replenishes energy storage.

4. Greek Yogurt and Fruit Parfait:

Choose a Greek yogurt parfait topped with various fruits and nuts or seeds. Greek yogurt has protein, fruits provide natural sugars and vitamins, and nuts and seeds give healthy fats and crunch.

5. Electrolyte Hydration:

After your exercise, rehydrate with water or an electrolyte-containing sports drink. Electrolytes restore what is lost via sweating and aid in recuperation.

Syncing Carb Cycling with Different Workout Types

1. Muscular Strength Training:

Include high-carb days before or after weight training sessions. Carbohydrates provide you with the energy you need to lift heavier weights and build your muscles. Protein consumption is also crucial after an exercise to help with muscle regeneration.

2. Cardiovascular Exercise:

On days with moderate or high carbohydrate intake, engage in moderate- to high-intensity aerobic activities. Carbohydrates give the energy required for long-term aerobic exertion, while protein aids in muscle upkeep.

3. HIIT (High-Intensity Interval Training):

Combine high-intensity interval training with days with high or moderate carbohydrate intake. Carbohydrates provide energy for short spurts of activity, but low-carb days may be properly positioned for recuperation.

4. Active Rehabilitation:

On active recovery days, choose low- or moderate-carbohydrate options such as mild yoga, stretching, or walking. These days, fewer carbs are required to maintain muscle regeneration and general well-being.

5. CrossFit or functional training:

High-carb days should be planned around rigorous CrossFit or functional training sessions. Carbohydrates are essential for these exercises' intense motions and high-energy needs.

6. Endurance Training:

Plan high or moderate carb days for longer endurance workouts like long-distance running or cycling. Carbohydrates give long-lasting energy for strenuous activity.

7. Days of Rest and Regeneration:

When your body wants less energy, set aside low-carb or rest days. If weight reduction is your objective, this technique encourages fat use and helps you sustain a calorie deficit.

CHAPTER FIVE

OVERCOMING PLATEAUS AND CHALLENGES

Recognizing Common Plateaus

Recognizing frequent plateaus in your fitness and nutrition journey is critical for overcoming obstacles and continuing your progress. Plateaus occur when there is no discernible change or progress, despite your efforts. You can remain motivated, change your strategy, and push through hurdles by identifying and resolving these plateaus.

1. Recognizing Stagnation:

Recognizing a plateau entail recognizing when your development slows or stops. This might be in the form of weight reduction, strength increases, increased energy, or other fitness-related objectives.

2. Frustration Avoidance:

Plateaus may be unpleasant and demotivating, but accepting them as a normal part of the trip can help you have a good attitude. Instead of becoming disheartened, you see them as possibilities for development.

3. Assessment and Adaptation:

When you see a plateau, you should reconsider your present approach. This review may include an examination of your fitness program, eating plan, sleep habits, stress levels, and other factors.

4. Plateau Origins:

Adaptability (your body grows adapted to your routine), insufficient intensity or diversity, poor recuperation, and, in rare cases, overtraining are all common reasons for plateaus.

5. Changing Variables:

Once the reason for a plateau has been identified, factors may be adjusted to drive development once again. This might imply altering your training program, boosting or adjusting your carb cycling strategy, or implementing new recuperation tactics.

6. Setting New Objectives:

Plateaus provide a chance to establish new objectives or refocus your efforts. If your weight reduction plateaus, you might shift your attention to boosting your strength or endurance.

7. Seeking Professional Help:

Recognizing a plateau may indicate that it is time to seek the advice of a fitness trainer, nutritionist, or other specialist. They may provide crucial insights and advice to help you break through the plateau.

8. Data Tracking and Analysis:

Looking at data, like exercise records, meal journals, and progress images, might help you identify plateaus. These records include unbiased information on your travels.

9. Psychological Resilience:

Overcoming plateaus strengthens psychological resilience and fosters a development mentality. You learn to adapt and persevere in the face of adversity.

10. Experimentation and Learning:

Plateaus foster experimentation. Experimenting with various routines, diets, or recuperation techniques might help you learn more about your body's reactions and preferences.

11. Long-Term Success:

You learn the skills and tactics required for long-term success by successfully detecting and managing plateaus. You recognize that growth is not always linear, but with perseverance, you can reach your objectives.

12. Non-Scale Victories to Be Celebrated:

Recognizing plateaus enables you to rejoice in non-scale wins. These triumphs might include gains in strength, flexibility, mood, or general well-being.

Strategies to Break Plateaus

1. Modify nutritional intake

- **Caloric Control:** Examine your calorie intake. Your body may have adapted if you've been in a calorie deficit for a long time. To restart progress, consider changing your calorie intake slightly.

- **Carb Cycling Alternatives:** Change the proportion of high, moderate, and low carb days in your carb cycling strategy. This might jolt your metabolism and inspire transformation.

2. Review Your Exercise Routine:

- **Change Exercise Choice:** Change up your workouts or try new ones. Repetitive exercises might cause your body to adapt, resulting in plateaus.

- **Increase Intensity:** Increase the intensity of your exercises gradually. Lifting heavier weights, increasing repetitions, or decreasing rest times may all help.
- **Different Rep Ranges:** Alter your rep ranges on a regular basis. If you've been performing high repetitions, try switching to lower reps with heavier weights.

3. Employ progressive overload:

Gradual Progression: Aim to gradually increase the weight, repetitions, or sets throughout your exercises. This promotes muscle development and adaptability.

Mind-Muscle Connection: Concentrate on the consistency of your repetitions. An improved mind-muscle connection ensures that muscle groups are adequately targeted.

4. Improve Recovery:

- **Sleep Quality:** Make sure you're receiving enough quality sleep. Sleep is essential for muscle healing and general health.
- **Days of Rest:** Rest days should not be underestimated. Allow your body to fully heal.

- **Active Rehabilitation:** On rest days, include mild exercises such as walking, stretching, or yoga to enhance blood flow and mobility.

5. Nutrition and Hydration Timing:

- **Hydration:** Drink plenty of water before, during, and after exercises. Dehydration may have an effect on performance and recuperation.
- **Pre-Exercise Nutrition:** Fuel your workouts with a well-balanced breakfast or snack that contains both carbohydrates and protein. This helps with energy and muscle restoration.
- **Nutrition Post-Workout:** Consume a protein-carbohydrate blend after exercises to help with muscle repair and replace glycogen levels.

6. Stress Management and Lifestyle Factors:

- **Stress Reduction:** Chronic stress may stymie advancement. Use stress-reduction strategies such as meditation, deep breathing, or activities that you love.
- **Balanced Lifestyle:** Make sure your way of life supports your fitness objectives. Adequate sleep, good relationships, and general well-being all help.

7. Maintain Patience and Consistency:

Attitude: Plateaus are both natural and transient. Maintain a positive attitude and concentrate on the long-term journey rather than the short-term outcomes.

Continuity: Consistency is essential. Stick to your strategy, make modifications as required, and trust the process.

8. Seek Professional Help:

Seek the advice of a trainer or a nutritionist: If you're having trouble breaking through a plateau, seek counsel from specialists who can give tailored advice based on your specific circumstances.

Adapting Carb Cycling for Long-Term Success

1. Begin slowly:

Begin with a low-carb diet, gradually integrating higher and lower-carb days. This assists your body in adjusting and avoiding overload.

2. Pay Attention to Your Body:

Take note of how your body reacts to varied carbohydrate amounts. Energy levels, emotions, and performance may all provide information about what works best for you.

3. Experiment and fine-tune:

Carb cycling is not a one-size-fits-all activity. Experiment with various carb cycling tactics, frequencies, and day types. Adjust according to what produces the greatest outcomes.

4. Make Whole Foods a Priority:

Your carbohydrate sources should be nutrient-dense whole foods. To improve general health, eat more veggies, fruits, whole grains, and legumes.

5. Preparation and Planning:

Plan your meals and snacks ahead of time to ensure you reach your carbohydrate and nutritional targets. Preparation keeps you on track, even on hectic days.

6. Accept Flexibility:

Allow for some leeway in your carb cycling strategy. If an unforeseen occasion or urge occurs, alter your carb consumption without feeling guilty.

7. Mindfully Incorporate Treats:

Include goodies on occasion, but do so with caution. On higher-carb days, you may allow yourself a tiny pleasure without jeopardizing your progress.

8. Maintain Hydration:

Hydration is critical. Drink enough water throughout the day to aid digestion, energy levels, and general health.

9. Track Progress:

Keep track of your progress throughout the year. Changes in weight, energy, strength, and other indicators should be noted. Based on your observations, modify your strategy.

10. Honor non-scale victories:

Recognize changes that go beyond the scale, such as more energy, a better mood, better sleep, or improved physical performance.

11. Adapt to Changes in Your Life:

Life is ever-changing. Prepare to modify your carb cycling strategy as your exercise levels, objectives, and circumstances change.

12. Concentrate on Overall Health:

Remember that health is more than simply physical appearance. Along with your athletic objectives, prioritize your mental, emotional, and spiritual well-being.

13. Seek Professional Help:

Consult a trained nutritionist or fitness expert if you're unsure how to modify your carb cycling strategy or are experiencing difficulties. They may provide specific suggestions.

14. Keep a Positive Attitude:

Approach carb cycling with a positive mindset and a long-term outlook. Consistency and patience are essential for long-term success.

15. Accept Learning:

Continue to learn about nutrition, exercise, and how your body reacts to carb cycling. This information allows you to make more educated judgments.

CHAPTER SIX

MONITORING PROGRESS AND ADJUSTING

Tracking Your Carb Intake and Meals

Tracking your meals and carb consumption may help you stay accountable and ensure you're sticking to your carb cycling strategy exactly.

1. Food Journal:

Keep track of what you eat each day using a real notepad or a digital app.

Take note of the meal type, portion sizes, and projected macronutrient composition, including carbohydrates.

Include details on the carb cycling strategy you're using that day.

2. Nutrition Apps:

Log your meals using apps like MyFitnessPal, Chronometer, or Lose It! These applications often offer vast food databases that may help you quickly monitor carb consumption.

3. Portion Management:

To monitor your carb consumption, learn to estimate portion sizes visually.

Get acquainted with typical carb serving amounts to make tracking easier.

4. Carbohydrate Counting:

Learn to count carbohydrates for a more exact approach. This entails determining the carbohydrate content of each item you ingest.

For correct carb counts, consult nutrition labels or internet resources.

5. Meal Preparation:

Plan and prepare your meals ahead of time. This makes tracking your carb consumption easy since you know exactly what's in your meals.

6. Carbohydrate Cycling Apps:

Some applications are particularly developed for carb cycling. They may assist you in planning your high, moderate, and low carb days and tracking your consumption appropriately.

7. Digital Spreadsheets:

Make a digital spreadsheet to track your daily meals, snacks, and carb consumption. This may also assist you in tracking patterns over time and making necessary modifications.

8. Reading the Label:

Check the nutrition labels on packaged items to see how many carbs are in them.

Consider serving sizes and how they fit into your carb cycling strategy.

9. Seek the advice of a dietitian:

Consult a certified nutritionist if you're uncertain about measuring your carb consumption. They can help you precisely analyze your carbohydrate consumption and customize it to your specific requirements.

10. Mindful Eating:

While monitoring is beneficial, mindful eating should be prioritized. Take note of hunger and fullness signs and pay heed to your body's messages.

Measuring Body Composition Changes

Body composition changes may be used to measure your development and the efficacy of your training and dietary activities.

1. Body Dimensions:

Use a tape measure to measure crucial regions of your body on a regular basis. Waist, hips, chest, arms, and thighs are common locations.

Save these measures and compare them over time.

2. Weight on the Scale:

While weight is not the only measure of body composition, it may give insight into overall improvement. Keep in mind that water retention, muscle growth, and hormone variations may all have an impact on scale weight.

3. Percentage of Body Fat:

This is one of the most accurate approaches for monitoring body composition changes. Skinfold calipers, bioelectrical impedance scales, DEXA scans, and body fat scales are all methods for calculating body fat percentage.

4. Photos of Progress:

Take front, side, and back photographs on a regular basis in consistent lighting and attire.

Compare these photographs over time to see how muscle definition, body form, and overall composition change.

5. Clothing Dimensions:

Pay attention to how your clothes fit and feel. Clothing size and fit are often affected by changes in body composition.

6. Power and Performance:

Keep track of your strength and performance gains throughout the exercises. Increased weights, repetitions, or endurance may all suggest improvements in muscle mass and overall composition.

7. Changes in Body Circumference:

Track changes in certain body circumferences, such as waist and hip circumferences. Variations in these parameters may indicate changes in body composition.

8. Mirror Analysis:

While glancing in the mirror is subjective, it may give insight into changes in muscle definition, tone, and general physique.

9. Professional Evaluations:

Consider hiring a personal trainer or qualified dietician to do body composition exams for you.

10. Patience and Consistency:

Keep in mind that changes in body composition may not be quick. Your efforts must be consistent.

Track progress over weeks and months rather than days.

Making Informed Adjustments to Your Plan

Making informed revisions to your strategy is a critical skill for adjusting to changes, breaking through plateaus, and attaining long-term success.

1. Evaluate Your Progress:

Evaluate your progress toward your objectives on a regular basis. Weight, body composition, strength, energy levels, and general well-being are all affected.

2. Recognize patterns and plateaus:

Examine your success, or lack thereof, for trends. Identify any points where your results have stagnated or slowed.

3. Collect Information:

Gather information on your diet, exercise, sleep, stress levels, and any other aspects that may affect your development.

4. Examine Your Strategy:

Examine your current exercise and diet regimen. Take into account your carb cycling approach, training regimen, recuperation routines, and other factors.

5. Identify Modification Areas:

Identify particular aspects of your strategy that may need to be adjusted based on your evaluation and data. It might be your carbohydrate distribution, intensity of activity, meal time, or recuperation tactics.

6. Establish Specific Goals:

Define the goals you wish to accomplish with the changes. Clarity is essential when it comes to breaking through a plateau, increasing energy levels, or achieving a certain fitness objective.

7. Plan Alterations:

Make a thorough strategy for the changes you wish to make. This might include altering your carb cycling plan, modifying your training program, or experimenting with different recuperation strategies.

8. Implement gradual changes:

Implement adjustments gradually rather than making big changes all at once. This allows you to track the effect of each change.

9. Monitor Reactions:

Keep note of how your body reacts to the changes. Changes in energy, strength, mood, and general improvement should be noted.

10. Examine the Results:

Analyze the consequences of the alterations after a fair amount of time. Are you seeing any beneficial changes? Have you overcome any stumbling blocks?

11. Iterate and Learn:

Regardless of the result, you're learning something new. If the changes work, you've discovered an effective strategy. If not, you now know what doesn't work.

12. If necessary, make further adjustments:

Make any required revisions based on your findings. This might include fine-tuning the changes you've made or attempting entirely new tactics.

13. Seek Professional Help:

If you're unclear on how to change your plan, talk to a qualified nutritionist, personal trainer, or other fitness specialist.

14. Be consistent and patient:

Adapting your strategy needs patience and perseverance. Because not every change will provide instant benefits, remain dedicated to the process.

15. Accept the Journey:

Making educated changes is a necessary step toward long-term success. Accept the sense of learning and empowerment that comes with knowing your body's answers.

CHAPTER SEVEN

SUSTAINABILITY AND LIFESTYLE INTEGRATION

Carb Cycling as a Lifestyle, Not a Diet

The slogan "Carb Cycling as a Lifestyle, Not a Diet" stresses a change in mindset from seeing carb cycling as a short-term eating plan to accepting it as a long-term way of life.

1. Long-Term Strategy:

- **Diet vs. Way of Life:** Diets are often connected with short changes in eating habits in order to achieve a particular objective, while a lifestyle refers to a more permanent and comprehensive way of life.

2. Durability:

- **Diet Attitude:** Diets sometimes contain severe rules and limits that may be difficult to follow, resulting in a cycle of on-and-off eating behaviors.
- **Attitude toward Lifestyle:** Carb cycling as a lifestyle involves incorporating it into your daily routine in a manner that is both pleasurable and manageable in the long run.

3. Adaptability and Flexibility:

- **Diet Attitude:** Diets contain strict guidelines that might be difficult to follow in different settings or when living circumstances change.

- **Attitude toward Lifestyle:** Carb cycling as a way of life provides for adaptation and flexibility. Your approach may be modified depending on your tastes, activities, and changing objectives.

4. Long-Term Results:

- **Diet Attitude:** Diets often have short-term outcomes, and after the diet is over, there is a danger of relapsing to old habits and regaining lost weight.

- **Attitude toward lifestyle:** Carb cycling as a way of life offers steady improvement and long-term outcomes. It becomes a long-term method of managing weight, energy levels, and general well-being.

5. Emphasis on Health and Wellness:

Diet Attitude: Diets may occasionally emphasize quick weight reduction above long-term health and well-being.

Attitude toward lifestyle: When carb cycling is seen as a lifestyle, it has the ability to benefit not just physical objectives but also general health, mood, energy, and vitality.

6. Mindset Change:

Diet Attitude: Diets, by emphasizing limits and constraints, may promote a negative connection between food and body image.

Attitude toward lifestyle: Carb cycling as a way of life promotes a healthy and balanced relationship with food. While eating a variety of meals, you learn to make conscious choices that correspond with your objectives.

7. Ongoing Learning:

Diet Attitude: Diets often present a set of guidelines to follow without encouraging a more in-depth grasp of nutritional options.

Attitude toward Lifestyle: Embracing carb cycling as a lifestyle entails continual education about nutrition, how your body reacts to certain meals, and what works best for your specific requirements.

Socializing and Dining Out on Carb Cycling

With a little forethought and flexibility, socializing and eating out while carb cycling may be fun and feasible.

1. Plan ahead of time:

Before you go, look up the restaurant's menu online. This allows you to locate carb-friendly choices and plan your meal ahead of time.

2. Carbohydrate Selection:

Choose complex carbohydrates such as whole grains, veggies, and legumes. These give prolonged energy and are often higher in nutritional density.

3. Portion Management:

Be mindful of portion sizes. Because restaurants sometimes offer bigger amounts, try splitting dishes or asking for a half-size piece.

4. Personalize Your Order:

Do not be afraid to make changes to your order. To help limit your carb consumption, request substitutes, tweaks, or sauces or dressings on the side.

5. Concentrate on Protein: Choose protein-rich foods first since protein may help you feel full and pleased.

6. Mindfulness in Eating:

Eat mindfully, appreciating each meal and paying attention to hunger and fullness signs. This may help you avoid overeating.

7. Be Clear About Your Objectives:

When eating with friends or family, discuss your carb cycling objectives. They are likely to be understanding and helpful.

8. Moderation in Alcohol:

Drink in moderation if you prefer to drink. Alcohol includes empty calories and might interfere with your carb cycling strategy.

9. Dishes to Share:

Sharing appetizers, sides, or desserts with others allows you to try new things without overindulging.

10. If necessary, pre-eat:

If you're worried about carb-heavy restaurant alternatives, try having a small, balanced snack before you arrive to help suppress your hunger.

Practice Adaptability: Be flexible. Not every meal has to be completely aligned with your carb cycling strategy. It's

OK to indulge in a pleasure now and again and to make modifications as required.

12. Maintain Hydration:

Stay hydrated during the meal. This aids digestion and may help to avoid overeating.

13. Dessert Ideas:

If you want dessert, share it or go for something lighter like fruit or a little piece of dark chocolate.

14. Emphasize Fun:

Keep in mind that socializing and eating out are also about fun and connection. Don't obsess over every element of your dish.

15. Schedule Active Days:

If you know you'll be eating out, arrange your carb cycling to coincide with more active days when your body may be able to better use the carbohydrates.

Traveling and Carb Cycling

Traveling while carb cycling may be difficult, but with careful preparation and adaptability, you can effectively navigate diverse surroundings and stick to your plan.

1. Research ahead of time:

Research local eateries, grocery shops, and food alternatives. Knowing where to look for carb-friendly options may help with meal planning.

2. Bring snacks:

Pack portable, carb-friendly snacks for the trip. Nuts, nuts, jerky, protein bars, and cut-up veggies may all be quick and easy snacks.

3. Select High-Protein Meals:

When traveling, choose high-protein foods. Protein keeps you full and helps you achieve your carb cycling objectives.

4. Meal Planning:

If possible, schedule your meals ahead of time. Determine where you'll eat and what you'll order to stay on track with your carb cycling strategy.

5. Macronutrient Balance:

Aim for well-balanced meals rich in protein, healthy fats, and complex carbohydrates. This helps to maintain blood sugar levels and energy levels throughout the day.

6. Think about intermittent fasting:

Consider intermittent fasting on travel days if it is acceptable for your carb cycling strategy. This might make it easier to consume while on the go.

7. Maintain Hydration:

Stay hydrated by drinking lots of water on your travels. Dehydration may have an effect on energy levels and digestion.

8. Make wise airport decisions:

Many airports are increasingly providing healthier food alternatives. When dining at the airport, choose salads, grilled proteins, and vegetable-based entrees.

9. Reusable Containers:

If you're bringing your own food, make sure it's in reusable containers to keep it fresh and easy to carry.

10. Communicate Dietary Requirements:

When eating out, discuss your dietary choices and limits. Many sites allow change requests.

11. Be Prepared for Time Zone Changes:

Adjust your meal timing to fit with your carb cycling program if traveling between time zones.

12. Mindfully Consume Local Foods:

While sticking to your carb cycling diet is important, take advantage of the chance to explore local delicacies in moderation.

13. Make Use of Technology:

When traveling, use carb monitoring apps or nutrition databases to estimate the carbohydrate content of meals.

14. Be adaptable:

Traveling often entails unforeseen events. Be adaptive and make the best decisions possible given the situation.

15. Make rest and recovery a priority:

Traveling may be exhausting. To promote your overall well-being, prioritize sleep, water, and self-care.

CHAPTER EIGHT

SAMPLE MEAL PLANS AND RECIPES

High Carb Day Recipes

Breakfast:

1. Oatmeal Power Bowl:

- Cook oats with almond milk; top with mixed berries
- A sliced banana
- chopped nuts
- A drizzle of honey.

2. Whole-Grain Pancakes:

- Make pancakes using whole-grain flour. Serve with Greek yogurt
- Fresh fruit
- A sprinkle of chia seeds.

Lunch:

3. Quinoa Salad:

Mix cooked quinoa with diced vegetables, chickpeas, feta cheese, and a lemon vinaigrette.

4. Sweet Potato and Black Bean Burrito Bowl:

- Combine roasted sweet potatoes

- Black beans
- Brown rice
- Avocado
- Salsa
- A dollop of Greek yogurt.

Dinner:

5. Grilled Chicken and Brown Rice Stir-Fry:

- Sauté chicken
- A variety of colorful vegetables
- Cooked brown rice in a teriyaki sauce.

6. Pasta Primavera:

- Toss whole wheat pasta with a medley of sautéed vegetables
- A tomato-based sauce
- Grated Parmesan.

Snacks:

7. Fruit and Yogurt Parfait:

Layer Greek yogurt with mixed berries, granola, and a drizzle of honey.

8. Hummus and Veggie Platter:

- Serve hummus with carrot sticks

- cucumber slices
- Bell pepper strips
- Whole wheat pita.

Desserts:

9. Banana Nut Muffins:

- Bake muffins using whole wheat flour
- Ripe bananas
- Chopped nuts for added texture.

10. Mixed Berry Smoothie Bowl:

- Blend mixed berries
- Banana
- Greek yogurt
- A splash of almond milk, top with granola and additional berries.

Low Carb Day Recipes

Breakfast:

1. Spinach and Mushroom Omelets:

- Whip up an omelet with spinach
- Mushrooms
- A sprinkle of feta cheese for added flavor.

2. Greek Yogurt Parfait:

- Layer Greek yogurt with sliced almonds
- Chia seeds
- A few raspberries for a burst of color.

Lunch:

3. Grilled Chicken Salad:

- Top a bed of mixed greens with grilled chicken
- Sliced cucumber
- cherry tomatoes
- A light vinaigrette.

4. Cauliflower Rice Bowl:

- Swap out regular rice for cauliflower rice and top it with sautéed vegetables and your choice of protein.

Dinner:

5. Baked Salmon with Asparagus:

- Season salmon fillets with herbs and bake them alongside roasted asparagus for a simple yet satisfying dish.

6. Zucchini Noodles with Pesto:

- Use spiralized zucchini as a base and toss it with homemade or store-bought pesto sauce.

Snacks:

7. Cucumber and Hummus Bites:

- Slice the cucumber into rounds and top each with a small dollop of hummus and a sprinkle of paprika.

8. Cheese and Cherry Tomatoes:

- Pair cheese cubes (such as mozzarella or cheddar) with cherry tomatoes for a quick and tasty snack.

Desserts:

9. Berries and Whipped Cream:

- Enjoy a mix of fresh berries with a dollop of unsweetened whipped cream or Greek yogurt.

10. Dark Chocolate Almonds:

- Satisfy your sweet tooth with a few dark chocolate-covered almonds.

Snack and Dessert Ideas for All Days

Snack Suggestions:

1. **Mixed nuts:** A handful of mixed nuts, such as almonds, walnuts, and cashews, offer healthful fats as well as a delicious crunch.

2. **Greek Yogurt:** Enjoy a bowl of Greek yogurt with honey drizzled on top, almonds sprinkled on top, and fresh berries.

3. **Hard-Boiled Eggs:** Hard-boiled eggs are a handy, high-protein snack.

4. **Celery Sticks with Nut Butter:** For a crunchy and creamy treat, spread almond or peanut butter on celery sticks.

5. **Apple and Cheese Slices:** For a balanced snack, pear slices of your favorite cheese with crisp apple slices.

6. **Trail Mixture:** Make your own trail mix by combining nuts, seeds, dried fruits, and a few dark chocolate pieces.

7. **Berries and Cottage Cheese:** For a protein-rich and refreshing snack, combine cottage cheese with a handful of mixed berries.

8. **Veggies and Hummus:** For a filling snack, dip carrot sticks, cucumber slices, and bell pepper strips in hummus.

Dessert Recipes:

1. Berries with Whipped Cream: Add a dollop of whipped cream or Greek yogurt to a dish of mixed berries.

2. Dark Chocolate Covered Strawberries: For a tasty and antioxidant-rich treat, dip strawberries in melted dark chocolate.

3. Chia Seed Pudding: Use almond milk to make chia seed pudding and top with sliced almonds and a drizzle of honey.

4. Frozen Banana Bites: Slice bananas into bite-sized chunks, then dip in Greek yogurt and freeze for a creamy and refreshing dessert.

5. Cinnamon-Baked Apple: For a warm and aromatic dessert, core one apple, sprinkle with cinnamon, and bake until soft.

6. Yogurt Parfait: For a filling parfait, layer yogurt with granola, fresh fruit, and a sprinkling of almonds or seeds.

7. Coconut Chia Seed Parfait: For a creamy and textural dessert, stack coconut yogurt and chia seed pudding.

8. Dates Stuffed with Nut Butter: For a naturally sweet and delicious treat, fill pitted dates with almond or peanut butter.

CHAPTER NINE

EXPERT TIPS AND SUCCESS STORIES

Insights from Women Over 40 Who've Succeeded

Professional Advice for Successful Carb Cycling:

1. Plan Ahead: To prevent making impulsive eating decisions, prepare your meals and snacks ahead of time.

2. Listen to Your Body: Pay attention to how your body reacts to various carbohydrate levels and alter your strategy appropriately.

3. Remain Hydrated: Staying hydrated helps with digestion, energy levels, and general well-being.

4. Prioritize Whole Foods: For long-term energy and good health, prioritize nutrient-dense whole foods.

5. Consistency is Key: To get real benefits, stick to your carb cycling diet over time.

6. Personalize Your Approach: Tailor your carb cycling strategy to your specific requirements, level of exercise, and preferences.

7. Mindful Eating: Slow down and appreciate your meals while paying attention to hunger and fullness signs.

8. Celebrate non-scale victories: Recognize gains in energy, mood, sleep, and physical performance.

9. Remain Educated: Continue to study about diet, fitness, and how your body reacts to various tactics.

Women Over 40's Success Stories:

1. Tina, 45: Tina suffered from weight gain and fluctuating energy levels. She recovered her energy, shed weight, and ran her first half marathon after starting carb cycling.

2. Sarah, 48: Sarah fits carb cycling into her hectic schedule as a working parent. Her body composition, attitude, and general vigor all improved.

3. Cynthia, 42: Cynthia's weight reduction plateau was broken via carb cycling. She found new methods to fuel her body and learned to live a healthy existence.

Insights from Successful Women Over 40:

1. Patience pays off: It takes time to achieve success. Instead of focusing on instant results, be patient and concentrate on your growth.

2. Flexibility is Important: Life is unpredictably unexpected. When things don't go as planned, flexibility in your strategy helps you stay on target.

3. A Positive Attitude Is Everything: A good attitude is essential. Celebrate your accomplishments, no matter how little, and learn from your setbacks.

Common Mistakes to Avoid:

1. Excessive Carbohydrate Restrictions: Excessive carbohydrate restriction may result in poor energy levels and impair your exercise.

2. Skip Protein: Ensure that you obtain adequate protein to promote muscle development and general health.

3. Disregarding Recovery: Neglecting recovery routines might result in burnout and impede development. Make sleep and rest days a priority.

4. Ignoring micronutrients: Don't only think about carbohydrates. Make a well-balanced diet rich in vitamins and minerals a top priority.

5. Failure to Stay Hydrated: Dehydration may have an influence on your performance and general well-being. Consume plenty of water throughout the day.

6. Progress Comparison: Everyone's path is unique. Avoid comparing your development to that of others; instead, concentrate on your own objectives and improvements.

CONCLUSION

Finally, embracing carb cycling as a lifestyle for women over 40 may be a life-changing path toward optimum health, fitness, and well-being. Beyond the constraints of conventional diets, this approach acknowledges the dynamic essence of life. Carb cycling enables women to deliberately utilize the power of carbs while embracing flexibility, awareness, and individual adaptations. Keep the following essential lessons in mind as you begin your journey:

Change Your Mindset to a Lifestyle Mindset: Carb cycling goes beyond diets to become an intrinsic part of your everyday life. It's about nurturing your body and mind over time and cultivating habits that correspond with your objectives and beliefs.

Embrace Your Uniqueness: Because no two women are the same, your carb cycling diet should be tailored to your own requirements, tastes, and circumstances. Customization enables you to flourish and make educated decisions that are in tune with your body.

Patience and Consistency: To achieve your objectives, you must be consistent and patient. Celebrate your minor triumphs, learn from your losses, and embrace your incremental growth over time.

Thoughtful Decisions: Approach carb cycling mindfully. Listen to your body, pay attention to hunger and fullness signs, and eat with thankfulness. This mindful eating technique feeds both your body and your connection with food.

Holistic Health: Carb cycling promotes more than just physical transformations. It improves your mood, energy, and general health. Self-care, relaxation, and positive mental modifications that lead to a holistic feeling of health should be prioritized.

Flexibility and adaptability: Your carb cycling path, like life, is dynamic. Adaptability and flexibility help you negotiate a variety of situations, from social gatherings to travel, while remaining focused on your objectives.

Ongoing Learning: Education is a kind of empowerment. Keep up-to-date on diet, fitness, and how your body reacts. This information enables you to make educated choices that will improve your carb cycling experience.

Made in the USA
Middletown, DE
24 August 2024